DANGER
DANGER
HOT
HOT
SAUCE!

DANGER
DANGER
HOT
HOT
SAUCE!

TRY THESE RECIPES IF YOU DARE!

This edition published by Parragon Books Ltd in 2014 and distributed by

Parragon Inc.
440 Park Avenue South, 13th Floor
New York, NY 10016
www.parragon.com/lovefood

LOVE FOOD is an imprint of Parragon Books Ltd

ISBN 978-1-4723-2989-9

Printed in China

New recipes written by Beverly Le Blanc
Introduction and incidental text by Dominic Utton and Beverly Le Blanc
New photography by Mike Cooper
New home economy by Lincoln Jefferson
Additional design work by Sian Williams
Internal and jacket flap illustrations by Julie Ingham and Nicola O'Byrne

Notes for the Reader
This book uses standard kitchen measuring spoons and cups. All spoon and cup measurements are level unless otherwise indicated. Unless otherwise stated, milk is assumed to be whole, eggs are large, individual vegetables are medium, and pepper is freshly ground black pepper. Unless otherwise stated, all root vegetables should be peeled prior to using.

Garnishes, decorations, and serving suggestions are all optional and not necessarily included in the recipe ingredients or method. The times given are only an approximate guide. Preparation times differ according to the techniques used by different people and the cooking times may also vary from those given. Optional ingredients, variations, or serving suggestions have not been included in the time calculations.

Picture acknowledgments
The publisher would like to thank the following for permission to reproduce copyright material: Front and back cover illustrations courtesy of iStock; page 7: Christopher Columbus © De Agostini Picture Library/De Agostini /A. Dagli Orti; page 103: Chile on windowsill © Dorling Kindersley/Peter Anderson.

CONTENTS

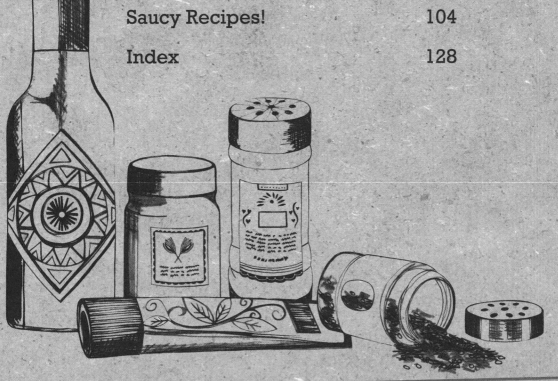

THE HISTORY OF CHILES

Everyone knows the rhyme: in 1492 Columbus sailed the ocean blue … Well, lovers of spicy food can add another line—he also found the chile, too! Before the discovery of the New World, the chile was a secret kept only by the South and Central Americans, where it had been used in their diet since 7500 BCE.

Columbus "discovered" the chile in the Caribbean and thought it simply another variety of sweet pepper. But although chile varieties were duly shipped back to Europe, the plants were viewed mostly as curiosities, with their heat occasionally being used for medicinal purposes.

Traders heading elsewhere from the Americas, however, found a different, more welcoming market. Chiles were brought to West Africa, where they immediately became a naturalized plant. And South Asia especially embraced the fiery flavors, incorporating chiles into their cuisine, perhaps because they were already familiar with pungent, spicy dishes but also because the plants were cheap to grow, meaning it was just as likely to be eaten by the common laborers as the aristocracy.

Gradually, the chile spread across all of Asia—and with the wonderful flavors came a host of superstitious beliefs about the properties of the potent little plant. It was believed they had the power to ward off the evil eye and most households would have a bunch of chiles hanging over the threshold to deter evil spirits. A handful of chiles mixed with ash from the hearth would also be waved over a man's head for good luck or to protect him from bad magic.

Although it took chiles just 50 years to spread from South America across the whole world, Europeans took longer to appreciate the taste. Spanish and Portuguese monks had started cooking with them during the mid-16th century, but the little vegetable with the big kick remained

a niche taste for much of the continent until the twentieth century.

So the next time somebody tells you chiles come from India, be sure to correct them—it took a European explorer to bring chiles to Asia in the first place.

THE HOT SAUCE BASICS

There's more to making a good hot sauce than just chopping up a couple of chiles. However, with a bit of judicious selection, common pantry ingredients can produce an astonishing variety of flavors and add complexity to your sauces. Try using the ingredients below, then experiment with quantities and varieties to make a customized version.

HERBS AND SPICES
Whether fresh or dried, these provide a depth of flavor. Jamaican Jerk Sizzling Sauce, for example, wouldn't taste authentic without dried allspice, and Chimichurri Sweltering Sauce relies on a medley of fresh herbs.

CHILES
The essential ingredient in most hot sauce recipes, these come in a wide range of varieties and heats.

OIL
Essential for frying chiles and other ingredients and for adding body to sauces. Keep a selection—sunflower, canola, peanut, olive—for a change of pace in flavors.

SALT
Always essential to bring out individual flavors.

SUGAR
White and brown sugars provide a counterpoint to hot spiciness and act as a preservative. Always dissolve sugar before bringing a sauce to a boil to prevent crystals from forming.

VINEGAR
Caribbean and many traditional North American sauces contain distilled white vinegar, but cider or red and white wine vinegars are also good. They provide a sour background, as well as acting as a preservative.

HOW TO HANDLE CHILES

It is the capsaicin in a chile that provides the heat and, as a rule, the smaller and thinner a chile is, the hotter it will taste (because it proportionally contains more seeds). All of a chile's capsaicin is produced in a gland running down the middle of the fruit and the seeds clustered around this part are the hottest part.

Be careful when you are chopping chiles, especially if you are removing the gland or the seeds. If your skin is sensitive, wear plastic gloves and never touch your eyes or mouth after handling chiles without first thoroughly washing your hands. You can also protect your hands by rubbing them first with vegetable oil, which acts as a barrier.

Pan-frying chiles can also release a potent vapor that may irritate your eyes, so set the extractor to high before starting or open a window. This is especially important when using the hot, hot, hot chiles in the Blow Your Head Off chapter!

Warning! The next time your mouth feels like it is on fire, don't drink a glass of water—that only spreads the heat around. Reach instead for milk or yogurt; dairy ingredients help to dilute the heat more effectively than anything else. It's not by chance that in India, for example, yogurt raita is always served with hot curries!

STORING HOT SAUCES

Some sauces, such as Searing Serrano & Cilantro, are best made just before serving and eaten immediately, but others made with fresh ingredients, such as Creole Gumbo Flamin' Sauce, will keep for up to two days in the refrigerator in an airtight container. Those with a lot of vinegar or sugar, such as Louisiana Hot Pepper Sauce, can be kept even longer—up to a month in the refrigerator. For longer storage, some sauces can be frozen or placed in sterilized jars. Each recipe in this book includes specific directions for storage.

FREEZING SAUCES

Always freeze sauces in small containers so you never defrost more than you need. After making the sauce, let cool to room temperature, then pour it into freezer-proof containers, leaving a ½-inch space at the top. Cover and label with the date. Most freezer-friendly sauces will freeze for up to a year, but they are best eaten within three months before the flavors dull. Thaw at room temperature to serve.

STERILIZING JARS

1. Only use jars made for preserving and never use jars with cracks or chips. Wash the jars and lids in hot, soapy water and rinse. If the recipe contains vinegar, use an acid-proof lid.

2. Place the jars upright in a heavy saucepan that is 2 inches deeper than the jars. Pour over enough boiling water to submerge the jars and boil for 15 minutes.

3. Use tongs to carefully remove the jars and let them drain on clean dish towels.

FILLING JARS FOR SHORT-TERM STORAGE

1. Use a funnel to pour the hot sauce into the hot jars. Leave a space of ½ inch between the sauce and the top of the jar. Wipe the rim, then secure the lid.

2. Let the sauce cool, then store in the refrigerator for up to a month. The length of time the sauce will last in the refrigerator depends on the vinegar and sugar content, so please see the storage information on the recipes for how long the sauce will last in the refrigerator.

USING A WATER BATH FOR LONGER STORAGE

1. For longer storage, use specific canning jars that have a two-part lid with a screw band, and fill as above. Position a rack in the bottom of a deep saucepan or use a canning kettle. Arrange the filled jars upright on the rack or in the kettle.

2. Pour over enough boiling water to fully submerge the jars, return the water to the boil and boil for 20 minutes for an 8-ounce jar or 30 minutes for a 1-pint jar if you live at or below 1,000 feet. Increase the time by 5 minutes if you live between 1,001 and 3,000 feet; by 10 minutes between 3,001 and 6,000 feet; by 15 minutes between 6,001 and 8,000 feet; and by 20 minutes between 8,001 and 10,000 feet.

3. Use tongs to remove the jars. Let cool to room temperature. If kept sealed, the jars will store for a year. Once opened, keep refrigerated and use for the amount of time stated in the recipe.

WARMING UP!

FEEL THE HEAT WITH THE SCOVILLE SCALE!

How do you measure the heat of a chile? With science, as it turns out!

In 1912, the American pharmacist Wilbur Scoville devised the Scoville Organoleptic Test (now simply called the Scoville Scale) to measure the piquancy, or hotness, of chiles. The heat of a chile comes from capsaicin, and the Scoville Scale measures how much capsaicin is present in any given chile.

Although technology has moved on in the 100 years since Scoville devised his method, his principles remain—and chiles are still measured according to his scale.

SCOVILLE HEAT UNITS	CHILE EXAMPLES
1,500,000-2,100,000	Trinidad Moruga Scorpion (the hottest known chile in the world)
855,000-1,463,700	Naga Viper, Infinity, Bhut Jolokia
350,000-855,000	Red Savina Habanero, Indian Tezpur
100,000-350,000	Habanero, Scotch Bonnet, Datil
50,000-100,000	Santaka, Chiltecpin, Peri Peri, Thai Chile
30,000-50,000	Cayenne, Tabasco, Pequin, Aji
15,000-30,000	Chile de Arbol
5,000-15,000	Yellow Wax, Serrano
2,500-5,000	Jalapeño, Mirasol, Chipotle, Poblano
1,500-2,500	Sandia, Cascabel
1,000-1,500	Pasilla, Anaheim, Ancho, Española
100-1,000	Pimento, Pepperoncini

KETCHUP
WITH A KICK

This is a great recipe for the time when tomatoes are at their cheapest and most plentiful. Make up large batches of this ketchup, following the storage instructions on page 10, and enjoy the taste of summer all year round.

MAKES: ABOUT 2½ CUPS   PREP TIME: 15 MINS   COOK TIME: 2¼ HRS

INGREDIENTS
5 pounds ripe, juicy tomatoes, coarsely chopped

2 red jalapeño chiles, coarsely chopped

1 sweet white onion, coarsely chopped

1 teaspoon salt, plus extra to taste

1 teaspoon fennel seeds

1 teaspoon black mustard seeds

1 cup cider vinegar or white wine vinegar

½ cup firmly packed light brown sugar

1 cinnamon stick

½ teaspoon ground nutmeg

½ teaspoon sweet paprika

1–3 teaspoons cayenne pepper, to taste

1–2 tablespoons tomato paste (optional)

pepper, to taste

1. Put the tomatoes, chiles, onion, and salt into a large saucepan over high heat. Stir until the tomatoes begin to break down, then reduce the heat to low, cover, and simmer for 30 minutes, or until the tomatoes are pulpy.

2. Meanwhile, put the fennel seeds and mustard seeds on a square of cheesecloth, bring together the sides, and tie to make a bag, then set aside.

3. Pass the tomato mixture through a strainer into a large saucepan, rubbing back and forth with a wooden spoon and scraping the bottom of the strainer to produce as much puree as possible.

4. Add the spice bag and the vinegar, sugar, cinnamon stick, nutmeg, paprika, and cayenne pepper. Season with pepper, then stir until the sugar dissolves. Bring to a boil, then reduce the heat and simmer, uncovered, for 1½ hours, skimming the surface as necessary, until the sauce is reduced and thickened. Transfer to a bowl and let cool.

5. Depending on how well-flavored the tomatoes were, you might want to add some tomato paste. Remove the spice bag and cinnamon stick.

6. Let the ketchup cool completely. Use the sauce immediately, or store it in an airtight container in the refrigerator for up to one month. For guidelines on longer storage, see page 10. You can also freeze the sauce for up to three months; see page 10.

BLAZING BARBECUE SAUCE

This is the perfect sauce to spice up any barbecue and tastes great when served with burgers, meat skewers, or chicken wings, fresh from the barbecue grill.

MAKES: ABOUT 1 CUP　　**PREP TIME: 5 MINS**　　**COOK TIME: 20 MINS**

INGREDIENTS

1 tablespoon olive oil

1 small onion, finely chopped

2–3 garlic cloves, crushed

1 red jalapeño chile, finely chopped

2 teaspoons tomato paste

1 teaspoon (or to taste) dry mustard

1 tablespoon red wine vinegar

1 tablespoon Worcestershire sauce

2–3 teaspoons packed light brown sugar

1¼ cups water

1. Heat the oil in a small, heavy saucepan, add the onion, garlic, and chile, and gently sauté, stirring frequently, for 3 minutes, or until beginning to soften. Remove from the heat.

2. Blend the tomato paste with the mustard, vinegar, and Worcestershire sauce to a paste, then stir into the onion mixture with 2 teaspoons of the sugar. Mix well, then gradually stir in the water. Add more sugar, if desired.

3. Return to the heat and bring to a boil, stirring frequently. Reduce the heat and gently simmer, stirring occasionally, for 15 minutes. Remove from the heat and let cool completely. Use the sauce immediately, or store it in an airtight container in the refrigerator for up to two weeks. For guidelines on longer storage, see page 10.

SWELTERING SWEET CHILI SAUCE

It can be tempting to reach for a store-bought jar of this dipping sauce when serving crisp Chinese egg rolls or wontons, but this is so easy to make, there's no reason to waste money on the commercial version.

MAKES: ABOUT ⅔ CUP　　**PREP TIME: 5 MINS**　　**COOK TIME: 25 MINS**

INGREDIENTS
4 red jalapeño chiles, halved

2 large garlic cloves, coarsely chopped

1½-inch piece fresh ginger, coarsely chopped

⅔ cup rice wine vinegar or cider vinegar

¾ cup superfine sugar or granulated sugar

⅔ cup water

2 tablespoons crushed red pepper flakes

¼ teaspoon salt

1. Put the chiles, garlic, and ginger into a small food processor and pulse until finely chopped but not pureed, scraping down the side as necessary. Alternatively, finely chop the chiles, garlic, and ginger with a sharp knife.

2. Add the vinegar, sugar, and water and blend together.

3. Transfer the ingredients to a heavy saucepan over high heat. Add the red pepper flakes and salt, stirring to dissolve the sugar.

4. Bring to a boil, without stirring. Reduce the heat to medium–low and simmer, stirring frequently so the sauce doesn't stick to the bottom of the pan, for about 20 minutes, or until thickened.

5. Transfer the sauce to a bowl and let cool completely, stirring occasionally. Use the sauce immediately, or store it in an airtight container in the refrigerator for up to two weeks. For guidelines on longer storage, see page 10.

PIQUANT PICO DE GALLO SAUCE

Hot and fresh flavors mingle in this simple Mexican salsalike sauce, which adds a burst of chile heat to everything from a bowl of tortilla chips to broiled meat and tacos.

MAKES: ABOUT ¾ CUP **PREP TIME: 10 MINS** **COOK TIME: NONE**

INGREDIENTS
⅔ cup tomato puree or tomato sauce

2 tablespoons freshly squeezed lime juice or orange juice, or to taste

2 large pickled garlic cloves or fresh garlic cloves, minced

½ sweet white onion, finely chopped

2 tablespoons pickled jalapeño chiles, drained and finely chopped

½ teaspoon ancho chili powder

small handful of cilantro leaves, finely chopped, to garnish

salt and pepper, to taste

1. Combine the tomato puree or sauce and lime juice in a nonmetallic bowl and season with salt and pepper. Add all the remaining ingredients, except the cilantro leaves.

2. The sauce can be served immediately, but will benefit from being left to stand at room temperature for 30 minutes for the flavors to blend. Stir well before serving and adjust the lime juice and salt and pepper, if necessary. Sprinkle with cilantro just before serving.

3. If there is any leftover sauce, pour a layer of olive oil over it, cover, and store in the refrigerator for up to three days. Stir in the oil just before serving and garnish with chopped fresh cilantro.

HERO TIPS

Still not hot enough? Use red or green Thai chiles instead of the jalapeños, or add ½ teaspoon Louisiana Hot Pepper Sauce (see page 80) for a real blast of heat.

ROASTING ROADHOUSE STEAK SAUCE

Savory and sweet with a blast of heat from the cayenne pepper, this rich sauce complements any steak it is paired with. It also makes a great marinade for pork chops.

MAKES: ABOUT 1½ CUPS   **PREP TIME: 10 MINS**   **COOK TIME: 50 MINS**

INGREDIENTS

1 (14½-ounce) can diced tomatoes
⅔ cup beef stock
4 garlic cloves, chopped
1 red onion, finely chopped
1 cup plus 2 tablespoons raisins
¼ cup Worcestershire sauce
1 tablespoon beef extract
1 tablespoon dry mustard, dissolved in 1 tablespoon water
2 tablespoons white wine vinegar
1 tablespoon light corn syrup
1 tablespoon packed dark brown sugar
½ teaspoon cayenne pepper
finely grated zest of 1 orange
salt and pepper, to taste

1. Mix together all the ingredients and season with salt and pepper in a heavy saucepan over high heat, stirring to dissolve the corn syrup and sugar. Bring to a boil, then reduce the heat to low and simmer, stirring freqently, for 30 minutes, or until the mixture is blended and the raisins fall apart.

2. Transfer the mixture to a blender or food processor and puree. Strain the mixture through a fine strainer into the cleaned pan, rubbing back and forth with a wooden spoon and scraping the bottom of the strainer to produce as much puree as possible.

3. Place the pan over medium heat and bring the puree to a boil. Reduce the heat to medium–low and simmer, uncovered, for 15 minutes, or until the sauce has thickened and reduced. Transfer to a bowl and let cool completely. Adjust the salt and pepper.

4. Use the sauce immediately, or store it in an airtight container in the refrigerator for up to three weeks. For guidelines on longer storage, see page 10.

SWELTERING SATAY SAUCE

The traditionally mild peanut sauce is heated up in this version with the addition of Indonesian chili paste (sambal oelek). It's sold in most Asian food stores but the intensity of the heat varies with the brand.

MAKES: ABOUT ¾ CUP **PREP TIME: 10 MINS** **COOK TIME: 5 MINS**

INGREDIENTS

2 tablespoons sunflower oil

2 shallots, finely chopped

1 large garlic clove, finely chopped

1-inch piece fresh ginger, finely chopped

1–3 teaspoons Indonesian chili paste (sambal oelek)

1 cup coconut milk

⅓ cup chunky peanut butter

1 teaspoon tamarind paste or freshly squeezed lime juice, or to taste

1 teaspoon dark soy sauce, or to taste

¼ cup water, if needed

4 red jalapeño chiles, seeded and thinly sliced

salt and pepper, to taste

1. Heat the oil in a wok over high heat until hot. Add the shallots, garlic, and ginger and stir-fry for 1–2 minutes, or until the shallots are soft and just beginning to brown. Stir in the chili paste, to taste, and continue cooking for an additional 30 seconds.

2. Add the coconut milk and peanut butter, stirring until blended. Stir in the tamarind paste and soy sauce, season with pepper, and continue stirring over medium heat for 2–3 minutes. If the mixture looks separated, stir in the water and beat well. Stir in the chiles. Adjust the seasoning, if necessary, and add extra chili paste, tamarind paste, and soy sauce.

3. Serve the sauce hot or at room temperature, or let cool completely and store it in an airtight container in the refrigerator for up to one week.

HERO TIPS

If using an unfamiliar brand of sambal oelek, start with the lesser amount and add the remaining chili paste at the end if the sauce isn't hot enough.

FIERY ROASTED TOMATO SAUCE

This sauce, with its paprika and sherry ingredients, has a Spanish flavor and is great when served as a dip with tortilla chips or as an accompaniment to Spanish omelet and fries.

MAKES: ABOUT ¾ CUP **PREP TIME: 10 MINS** **COOK TIME: 45 MINS**

INGREDIENTS

6 vine-ripened tomatoes
1 red bell pepper, cut into quarters and seeded
1 garlic clove, unpeeled
1 red onion, cut into quarters
¼ cup olive oil
1 small red jalapeño chile, minced
1 teaspoon hot paprika
1 tablespoon sherry
salt and pepper, to taste

1. Preheat the oven to 350°F.

2. Lay out the vegetables on a large baking pan, brush with olive oil, then roast in the oven, turning once halfway through cooking, for about 45 minutes or until they are blistered and slightly charred.

3. Let cool. When cool enough to handle, peel the tomatoes and red bell pepper, and squeeze the garlic from its skin. Transfer the tomato, red bell pepper, garlic flesh, and onion to a food processor and process to a fairly smooth consistency.

4. Spoon the mixture into a large serving bowl and stir in the chile, paprika, and sherry. Season with salt and pepper. Use the sauce immediately, or let cool completely and store it in an airtight container in the refrigerator for up to one week.

HERO TIPS

The tablespoon of sherry in this recipe can also be replaced by Madeira, which is a fortified wine from Portugal.

CREAMY BUT DEADLY MUSTARD SAUCE

The pale color of this sauce belies its hot flavor; this comes from the dry mustard with extra heat from the cayenne pepper—the heat kicks in at the back of the mouth and lingers after swallowing.

MAKES: ABOUT 1 CUP   **PREP TIME: 5 MINS**   **COOK TIME: 25 MINS**

INGREDIENTS

1 tablespoon olive oil

4 shallots, thinly sliced

1 large garlic clove, minced

2 tablespoons dry mustard

2 teaspoons cayenne pepper

1¼ cups beef stock, chicken stock, or vegetable stock

⅔ cup crème fraîche or sour cream

1 tablespoon whole-grain mustard

freshly squeezed lemon juice, to taste (optional)

salt and pepper, to taste

1. Heat the oil in a lidded skillet over medium heat. Add the shallots, cover with a piece of crumpled, wet wax paper, then cover the pan. Reduce the heat to low and let the shallots cook for 5–8 minutes, or until soft.

2. Uncover, remove the paper, and increase the heat. Add the garlic and stir for 1 minute. Stir in the dry mustard and cayenne pepper.

3. Slowly whisk in the stock, whisking constantly so the mustard doesn't form lumps. Bring to a boil and boil for 5–8 minutes, stirring continuously, until reduced by half.

4. Stir in the crème fraîche or sour cream and return to a boil. Reduce the heat and simmer for 10 minutes, or until reduced to a coating consistency. Stir in the whole-grain mustard and season with salt and pepper. Add 1–2 teaspoons of lemon juice, if using, to cut through the richness.

5. Serve the sauce immediately, or let it cool completely and stored in an airtight container in the refrigerator for up to two days. Reheat to serve.

29

HOT-AS-HELL HORSERADISH SAUCE

This quick and easy sauce gets its punchy heat from freshly grated horseradish. It's traditionally added to seafood cocktails, but a spoonful or two can be stirred into homemade tomato soup for an extra kick.

MAKES: ABOUT ⅔ CUP   **PREP TIME: 10 MINS**   **COOK TIME: NONE**

INGREDIENTS

½ cup ketchup, plus extra, if necessary

1-inch piece horseradish, finely grated, or 1 tablespoon grated horseradish

1 tablespoon freshly squeezed lemon juice, or to taste, plus extra, if needed

pepper, to taste

1. Put the ketchup and horseradish into a bowl and stir to combine.

2. Add the lemon juice and season with pepper. Stir to combine, then add extra lemon juice.

3. Serve the sauce immediately, or store it in an airtight container in the refrigerator for up to three weeks. After one or two days, the sauce will thicken, so you will need to beat in extra ketchup or lemon juice with a fork when ready to serve.

INTENSE ITALIAN ARRABBIATA SAUCE

Arrabbiata sauce is a classic Italian sauce and translates as "angry" in Italian, due to the fiery nature of the chiles. It is usually served as an accompaniment to pasta.

MAKES: ABOUT 2½ CUPS   **PREP TIME: 10 MINS**   **COOK TIME: 20 MINS**

INGREDIENTS

2 tablespoons olive oil

2 garlic cloves, chopped

1 red serrano chile, seeded and chopped

1 tablespoon grated lemon rind

4 ripe tomatoes, peeled and chopped

1 tablespoon tomato paste, blended with ⅔ cup water

pinch of sugar

1 tablespoon balsamic vinegar

1 tablespoon chopped fresh marjoram

pepper, to taste

1. Heat the oil in a heavy saucepan over medium heat, add the garlic and chile, and sauté, stirring continously, for 1 minute.

2. Sprinkle in the lemon rind and stir, then add the tomatoes with the blended tomato paste. Add the sugar and bring to a boil, then reduce the heat and simmer for 12 minutes. Season with pepper.

3. Add the vinegar and marjoram and simmer for an additional 5 minutes. Use the sauce immediately, or let it cool completely and store in an airtight container in the refrigerator for up to one week.

HERO TIPS

This sauce is best served with freshly cooked penne pasta. Spoon the sauce over the pasta and then sprinkle with parsley and Parmesan cheese.

KICKIN' CON CARNE SAUCE

Chili con carne sauce is a perennial favorite and the combination here of smoky ancho chili powder and hot, hot, hot cayenne pepper gives this version a great kick!

MAKES: ABOUT 2½ CUPS   PREP TIME: 10 MINS   COOK TIME: 20 MINS

INGREDIENTS

2 tablespoons sunflower oil

1 onion, finely chopped

1 red bell pepper, seeded and chopped

2 large garlic cloves, chopped

2 teaspoons ancho chili powder

2 teaspoons ground coriander

2 teaspoons ground cumin

1½ teaspoons cayenne pepper, or to taste

1 (14½-ounce) can diced tomatoes

1½ cups tomato puree or tomato sauce

1 tablespoon dried thyme, marjoram, or oregano

½ teaspoon sugar

salt and pepper, to taste

1. Heat the oil in a large skillet over medium–high heat. Add the onion and red bell pepper and sauté, stirring, for 3–5 minutes, or until soft. Add the garlic, chili powder, coriander, cumin, and cayenne pepper and stir for an additional minute.

2. Add the tomatoes, tomato puree or sauce, thyme, and sugar and season with salt and pepper. Bring to a boil, stirring, then reduce the heat so the liquid just bubbles and let cook for 15–20 minutes, until the sauce reduces by about half.

3. Transfer the sauce to a food processor or blender and puree.

4. Use the sauce immediately, or let it cool completely and store in an airtight container in the refrigerator for up to three days. You can freeze the sauce for up to three months; see page 10.

HERO TIPS

Double the quantities and have several portions of this in the freezer ready to make chili con carne to warm up winter evenings.

BLISTERING BEER & CHILI SAUCE

Fire up the heat of any barbecue with this sauce packed with chile flavor. Definitely a barbecue sauce for adults, with pale ale, molasses, and heat from cayenne pepper, ancho chili powder, and fresh jalapeño chiles replacing the sickly sweetness of so many barbecue sauces.

MAKES: ABOUT 2 CUPS   **PREP TIME: 10 MINS**   **COOK TIME: 45 MINS**

INGREDIENTS

2 tablespoons sunflower oil

1 red onion, finely chopped

1 tablespoon ancho chili powder

1½ teaspoons cayenne pepper

1 cup ketchup

¼ cup molasses

2 tablespoons packed dark brown sugar

2 teaspoons salt

¼ teaspoon pepper

1⅓ cups pale ale

2 tablespoons cider vinegar or red wine vinegar

2 tablespoons Worcestershire sauce

3 red, green, or mixed jalapeño chiles, chopped

1. Heat the oil in a saucepan over medium–high heat. Add the onion and sauté for 3–5 minutes, or until soft. Add the chili powder and cayenne pepper, then stir for 30 seconds. Add the remaining ingredients, except the chiles, stirring until the ketchup, molasses, and sugar are blended.

2. Bring to a boil, skimming the surface, if necessary. Add the chiles. Reduce the heat and let gently simmer, skimming the surface, if necessary, and stirring occasionally, for about 30 minutes, or until the sauce has a coating consistency.

3. Transfer the sauce to a food processor or blender and puree. Pass the mixture through a strainer, rubbing back and forth with a wooden spoon and scraping the bottom of the strainer to produce as much puree as possible.

4. Use the sauce immediately, or let it cool completely and store in an airtight container in the refrigerator for up to two weeks. For guidelines on longer storage, see page 10.

TASTE BUDS-ON-FIRE THAI GREEN SAUCE

With this sauce in the refrigerator, you will be enjoying a delicious curry with all the flavors of Thailand in no time! This sauce is especially good when used in poultry or vegetable curries.

MAKES: ABOUT 1½ CUPS   PREP TIME: 10 MINS   COOK TIME: 15 MINS

INGREDIENTS

2 tablespoons sunflower oil

1¾ cups coconut milk

1 tablespoon Thai fish sauce, or to taste

fresh lime juice, to taste

pepper, to taste

THAI GREEN CURRY PASTE

6 green Thai chiles, stems removed, coarsely chopped

4 fresh cilantro sprigs

4 scallions, chopped

2 green serrano chiles, chopped

2 garlic cloves, chopped

2 lemongrass stalks, outer layer removed, chopped

1 kaffir lime leaf, or the finely grated zest of 1 lime

1-inch piece fresh ginger, chopped

1 tablespoon sunflower oil

1 teaspoon ground coriander

1. To make the green curry paste, put all the ingredients into a food processor or blender and puree until a thick paste forms.

2. Heat the oil in a wok or saucepan over high heat. Add the curry paste and stir for 4–5 minutes, or until you can smell the aroma.

3. Stir in the coconut milk and fish sauce and season with pepper. Reduce the heat and simmer, stirring occasionally, for 10 minutes, until the flavors have blended and the sauce is reduced. Add the lime juice and adjust the fish sauce and pepper, if needed.

4. Use the sauce immediately, or let it cool completely and keep in an airtight container in the refrigerator for up to three days.

RED-HOT GARLIC & CHILI OIL

Chili oil can be used to spice up a huge range of dishes, from drizzling over pizzas or pasta to adding a splash to a Mexican-style beef chili. The longer you leave the oil to settle, the hotter it gets!

MAKES: ABOUT 1 CUP   **PREP TIME: 5 MINS**   **COOK TIME: 2 HRS**

INGREDIENTS
5 garlic cloves, halved lengthwise

2 tablespoons seeded and chopped jalapeño chile

1 teaspoon dried oregano

1 cup canola oil

1. Preheat the oven to 300°F. Combine the garlic, chile, and oregano with the oil in an ovenproof glass measuring cup or bowl. Place on a glass pie plate in the center of the oven and heat for 1½–2 hours. The temperature of the oil should reach 250°F.

2. Remove from the oven, let cool, then strain through cheesecloth into a clean jar. Store in an airtight container in the refrigerator for up to one month. You can also leave the garlic and chile pieces in the oil and strain before using.

HERO TIPS

Be very careful during the heating of the oil stage in Step 1 of this recipe. Make sure to use an ovenproof measuring cup or bowl and use thick oven mitts to carefully remove the oil from the oven when it reaches the desired temperature.

FEELING HOT, HOT, HOT!

IT'S GETTING HOT IN HERE!

Chiles can be deceptive little things—and some of the hottest chiles in the world don't look too fierce at all from the outside. Cut them open, however, and a fascinating anatomy is revealed …

CALYX
The structural base of the chile—and the point from which it flowers on the plant.

PEDUNCLE
Essentially, a fancy name for the stem. You don't eat this part.

EXOCARP
The protective layer of skin, or peel, around the chile.

SEEDS

Contrary to popular myth, these are not the hottest part of the chile—though their position next to the capsaicin gland (below) means they do absorb much of the heat from there.

PLACENTA

As you might guess by the name, this is the source of the biological growth of the chile—from the seeds inside to the fruit itself. Depending on the variety of chile, this can be white, yellow, or red.

MESOCARP

This fleshy layer protects the inside of the chile, and it also provides structural support.

CAPSAICIN GLAND

This is where the hotness comes from. Running from the placenta down the length of the chile, this gland produces capsaicin, the source of all chile heat.

ENDOCARP

The inside of the chile, it contains some heat due to its closeness to the capsaicin gland.

CHIPOTLE & LIME INFERNO SAUCE

Morita chipotle chiles and crushed red pepper flakes give this sauce a smoky flavor, reminiscent of foods grilled over wood chips, with a good hit of heat. The zingy lime adds a refreshing finish to the strong flavors. This is a good sauce to use in any slow-cooked meat dish.

MAKES: ABOUT 1¼ CUPS

PREP TIME: 10 MINS PLUS MATURING

COOK TIME: 10 MINS

INGREDIENTS
¼ cup sunflower oil or canola oil

1 white onion, finely chopped

2 large garlic cloves, crushed

1 teaspoon ground cinnamon

½ teaspoon ground allspice

½ teaspoon ground cumin

8 dried chipotle, morita, or meco chiles, or a combination, toasted and soaked (see page 82), stems removed and the soaking water reserved

1 tablespoon crushed red pepper flakes

1 teaspoon dried Mexican oregano or dried marjoram

1 teaspoon dried thyme

finely grated zest of 1 large lime

2 tablespoons freshly squeezed lime juice, or to taste

salt and pepper, to taste

1. Heat the oil in a skillet over medium heat. Add the onion and sauté, stirring, for 3–5 minutes, or until soft. Add the garlic, cinnamon, allspice, and cumin and sauté for an additional minute. Transfer to a food processor or blender.

2. Coarsely chop the chiles and add them to the food processor with the red pepper flakes, oregano, and thyme and season with salt and pepper. Puree until a paste forms, scraping down the sides. Add 1–2 tablespoons of the soaking liquid and process until a soft, thick sauce forms.

3. Pour the sauce into the pan and bring to a boil, stirring. Boil for 2–3 minutes, or until thick. Stir in the lime zest and lime juice. Adjust the seasoning, if necessary, and add extra juice, if desired.

4. The sauce is now ready to use, but is best to let cool completely and store in an airtight container in the refrigerator for at least one day. It will keep for up to two weeks in the refrigerator. For guidelines on longer storage, see page 10.

CREOLE GUMBO FLAMIN' SAUCE

Louisiana gumbos can be mild or spicy hot, and this sauce is one for heat lovers. Green Thai chiles are added to the "holy trinity" of Creole kitchens—celery, onion, and green or red bell peppers—with an extra burst of heat from cayenne pepper.

MAKES: ABOUT 2½ CUPS   **PREP TIME: 10 MINS**   **COOK TIME: 1¼ HRS**

INGREDIENTS

¼ cup sunflower oil or corn oil

¼ cup all-purpose flour

2 celery stalks, finely chopped

1 large onion, finely chopped

1 green bell pepper, chopped

1 red bell pepper, chopped

4 large garlic cloves, crushed

2 green Thai chiles, minced

1 teaspoon cayenne pepper

1 teaspoon smoked sweet paprika

3 cups chicken stock

1 (14½-ounce) can diced tomatoes

1 pound okra, thinly sliced

2 bay leaves

1 teaspoon salt

1 teaspoon dried thyme

½ teaspoon dried marjoram

pinch of pepper

½ teaspoon Louisiana Hot Pepper Sauce (see page 80) or other hot sauce (optional)

1. Heat the oil in a large saucepan over medium-high heat. Slowly whisk in the flour, whisking continuously to prevent lumps from forming. Cook the mixture, whisking, for about 10 minutes, or until it turns a dark hazelnut color.

2. Add the celery, onion, and green and red bell peppers, then reduce the heat and stir for 5–8 minutes, or until the vegetables are soft. Stir in the garlic, chiles, cayenne pepper, and paprika and cook for an additional minute.

3. Add the stock, tomatoes, okra, bay leaves, salt, thyme, marjoram, and pepper. Cover and bring to a boil, then reduce the heat and let simmer for about 1 hour, or until the sauce thickens. Adjust the pepper, if necessary, and stir in the hot sauce if the sauce isn't fiery enough.

4. Use the sauce immediately, or let it cool completely and store in an airtight container in the refrigerator for up to two days. You can freeze the sauce for up to one month; see page 10.

FEEL-THE-HEAT HARISSA SAUCE

For this sauce, use whatever hot chiles are available—the color of the sauce will range from flame red to a devilish brownish red, depending on the chiles used. After several days, the covering oil will have absorbed some of the heat and is great for using in salad dressings.

MAKES: ABOUT ¾ CUP **PREP TIME: 5 MINS PLUS SOAKING** **COOK TIME: 1-2 MINS**

INGREDIENTS

12 hot dried red chiles, such as aji, guajillo, New Mexican, or pasilla, or a combination

1 tablespoon Aleppo crushed red pepper flakes

½ cup olive oil, plus extra, if needed

1 teaspoon caraway seeds

1 teaspoon cumin seeds

½ teaspoon fennel seeds

2 red jalapeño chiles, finely chopped

salt and pepper, to taste

1. Put the dried chiles into a heatproof bowl, pour boiling water over them to cover, and let stand for 15 minutes. Drain well and pat dry. When cool enough to handle, remove the stems and finely chop the chiles.

2. Transfer to a bowl and add the red pepper flakes and oil. Set aside for 1 hour.

3. Meanwhile, heat a dry skillet over medium–high heat. Add the caraway seeds, cumin seeds, and fennel seeds and dry-fry for 1–2 minutes, or until aromatic. Transfer the seeds to a mortar and finely grind with a pestle.

4. Transfer the soaked chile mixture, ground seeds, and chopped fresh chiles to a small food processor or blender. Season to taste, then puree. Adjust the seasoning if necessary. Slowly add more oil, if necessary, to make a thick sauce.

5. Use the sauce immediately, or store it with a layer of olive oil poured over the surface, in an airtight container in the refrigerator for up to two weeks.

INTENSE TEXAN CHILI SAUCE

Texan chili—or Big Red as the locals know it—is not made with beans, just meat, so it needs a tasty sauce, such as this version with plenty of heat and flavor. This sauce can also be used in other chili recipes that are made with kidney beans and vegetables.

MAKES: ABOUT 3 CUPS   **PREP TIME: 10 MINS**   **COOK TIME: 30 MINS**

INGREDIENTS

2 tablespoons sunflower oil or canola oil

1 red onion, chopped

2 large garlic cloves, chopped

1 green serrano chile, halved lengthwise

1 tablespoon packed dark brown sugar

2 teaspoons ground cumin

2 teaspoons dried Mexican oregano or dried thyme

2 dried morita chipotle chiles, toasted, soaked, seeded, and chopped (see page 82)

1 dried guajillo chile, toasted, soaked, seeded, and chopped (see page 82)

1 dried New Mexico red chile, toasted, soaked, seeded, and chopped (see page 82)

1 (14½-ounce) can diced tomatoes

½ cup beef stock

½ cup strong black coffee

salt and pepper, to taste

1. Heat the oil in a saucepan over medium–high heat. Add the onion and sauté for 3–5 minutes, or until soft. Add the garlic, serrano chile, sugar, cumin, and oregano and sauté for another minute.

2. Transfer the onion mixture to a food processor or blender. Add the chipotle chiles, guajillo chile, and New Mexico chile, tomatoes, stock, and coffee and season with salt and pepper. Process until pureed, scraping down the sides, if necessary.

3. Transfer the puree to the pan and bring to a boil. Reduce the heat to low, cover, and simmer for 15 minutes, stirring occasionally. Adjust the seasoning, if necessary.

4. Use the sauce immediately, or let it cool completely and store it in an airtight container in the refrigerator for up to three days. You can freeze the sauce for up to three months; see page 10.

CHIMICHURRI SWELTERING SAUCE

No Latin American barbecue is complete without a bowl of zingy, fresh chimichurri, a blend of herbs and chiles. This hot and spicy version has a Thai chile to crank up the heat. Serve with all grilled and roasted meats or serve with a selection of vegetable sticks.

MAKES: ABOUT ¾ CUP **PREP TIME: 5 MINS PLUS MARINATING** **COOK TIME: NONE**

INGREDIENTS
¾ cup fresh cilantro leaves

½ cup fresh flat-leaf parsley leaves

4 garlic cloves, coarsely chopped

1–2 green Thai chiles, finely chopped

1 teaspoon dried red pepper flakes

1 teaspoon dried Mexican oregano or dried thyme (optional)

½ cup sunflower oil or canola oil

¼ cup red wine vinegar or white wine vinegar

salt and pepper, to taste

1. Put the cilantro, parsley, garlic, chiles, red pepper flakes, oregano, if using, into a food processor, season with salt and pepper, and finely chop, scraping down the sides, if necessary. Do not blend to a puree.

2. With the motor running, slowly drizzle in the oil. Add the vinegar and adjust the seasoning, if necessary.

3. Use the sauce immediately, but it is best if stored it in an airtight container in the refrigerator for at least three hours to let the flavors blend. The sauce will keep for up to three days in the refrigerator if covered with an extra layer of oil, although its bright green color will dull. Drain off the oil before serving the sauce.

HERO TIPS

If you don't want to use a food processor, finely chop the cilantro, parsley, and garlic, then mix together in a nonmetallic bowl.

RED-HOT GREEN SAUCE

Tortilla chips with store-bought salsa will seem mild and boring once you've tried this sauce, which is packed full of punch with pickled jalapeños and hot smoked paprika. It's zesty and hot, and the fresh green color looks appetizing in a contrasting bowl.

MAKES: ABOUT 1¾ CUPS   **PREP TIME: 10 MINS**   **COOK TIME: NONE**

INGREDIENTS

1½ (11-ounce) cans tomatillos, drained, stem ends removed, and coarsely chopped

4 scallions, chopped

2 large garlic cloves, coarsely chopped

2 tablespoons drained pickled jalapeño chiles, chopped

handful of cilantro leaves, plus extra, finely chopped, to garnish

freshly squeezed lime juice, to taste

honey, to taste

½ teaspoon hot smoked paprika

salt and pepper, to taste

1. Put the tomatillos, scallions, garlic, chiles, and cilantro leaves into a food processor and process in short blasts to finely chop but not puree.

2. Transfer the mixture to a bowl. Season with salt and pepper, then add lime juice and honey. Stir in the paprika.

3. Use the sauce immediately, or store it in an airtight container in the refrigerator for up to four days, although the color will start to dull after three days. Sprinkle with chopped cilantro just before serving.

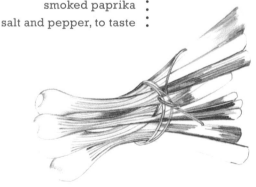

58

SPICE UP YOUR LIFE!

Chiles are only one way to add heat to your food. Why not check out some of these other spices and pastes that flavor hot sauce recipes around the globe?

HARISSA PASTE

There are many variations of this dark red paste, which adds heat and flavor to food in North Africa. The constant ingredients are chiles, oil, and caraway seeds. Make your own (see page 52) or buy it in larger supermarkets or Middle Eastern food stores.

HORSERADISH

This thick, white root has an intense, sharp, and hot flavor when it is freshly grated. Mixing grated horseradish with lemon juice helps prolong the sharpness. If buying grated horseradish, avoid horseradish sauce, which is mixed with cream, or grated horseradish in vinegar.

MUSTARD

Choose bright yellow dry mustard in powder form for the hottest flavor in a sauce. To prevent lumps from forming, treat it like flour and stir any liquids into it.

PAPRIKA

Produced in Hungary, but also in Spain and many other countries, paprika is the finely ground powder of sweet peppers. Its heat ranges from mild and sweet to intensely hot. Spanish pimentón is paprika made from dried and smoked peppers.

SAMBAL OELEK PASTE

From Southeast Asia, this red sauce, made with chiles, salt, and citrus juice or vinegar, comes in varying degrees of hotness. It is sold in supermarkets and specialty food stores.

SICHUAN PEPPERCORNS

The flavor of these rosy brown dried peppercorns is unmistakable— the heat blends with a lingering tingling sensation on your tongue and cheeks.

WASABI

Known as Japanese horseradish, pale green wasabi comes from a root and packs a real punch. It is pungent and hot, and sold already prepared as a paste or in powder form.

TRY-IT-IF-YOU-DARE THAI RED CURRY SAUCE

Although store-bought red curry pastes are bright red, the homemade pastes tend to be much paler in color. This recipe includes Kashmiri chili powder or hot paprika, as much for the redness that they impart as for their heat.

MAKES: ABOUT 2 CUPS　　**PREP TIME: 30 MINS**　　**COOK TIME: 10 MINS**

INGREDIENTS
2 tablespoons sunflower oil

1¾ cup coconut milk

1 tablespoon Thai fish sauce, or to taste

1 tablespoon freshly squeezed lime juice, or to taste

1 tablespoon dark soy sauce, or to taste

4 fresh red or green Thai chiles, thinly sliced

pepper, to taste

RED CURRY PASTE
24 dried Thai chiles, stems removed

2 large garlic cloves, chopped

2 large shallots, chopped

1 lemongrass stalk, chopped

1-inch piece fresh ginger, finely chopped

1-inch piece galangal (or extra ginger), coarsely chopped

2 teaspoons Kashmiri chili powder or hot paprika

2 teaspoons ground coriander

1 teaspoon ground cumin

1. To make the curry paste, soak the chiles in hot water to cover for 20 minutes, or until soft, weighing them down with a small heatproof plate.

2. Strain, reserving the liquid, then chop the chiles and put them into a small food processor.

3. Add the remaining paste ingredients and puree, scraping down the sides and adding a little of the reserved liquid, if necessary, until a thick paste forms.

4. Heat the oil in a wok over high heat. Add 3 tablespoons of the curry paste and stir for 30 seconds. Stir in the coconut milk, fish sauce, lime juice, and soy sauce, season with pepper, and bring to a boil, stirring. Reduce the heat and simmer for 5 minutes. Stir in the chiles. Adjust the curry paste, fish sauce, lime juice, soy sauce, and pepper, if necessary.

5. Use the sauce immediately, or let it cool completely and store it in an airtight container in the refrigerator for up to three days.

SEARING SERRANO & CILANTRO SAUCE

This can be made either smooth, like mayonnaise, in a food processor, or chunkier, like guacamole, by hand. Either way, it's great for adding a kick to pan-fried seafood or as an alternative to guacamole in tacos and burritos.

MAKES: ABOUT 1 CUP   **PREP TIME: 10 MINS**   **COOK TIME: NONE**

INGREDIENTS
⅓ cup sunflower oil

3 tablespoons freshly squeezed lime juice, or to taste

1 teaspoon honey, or to taste

1 soft, ripe avocado, coarsely chopped

2 red or green Serrano chiles, seeded and coarsely chopped

½-inch piece fresh ginger, finely grated

small handful cilantro leaves, coarsely chopped

salt and pepper, to taste

1. Put 3 tablespoons of the oil, the lime juice, and honey in a small food processor, season wtih salt and pepper, and blend. Add the avocado and the remaining oil and process until blended, scraping down the sides as necessary.

2. Add the chiles, ginger, and cilantro leaves to the food processor and process, in short blasts, until the chiles and cilantro are finely chopped and distributed through the sauce.

3. Alternatively, put 3 tablespoons of the oil, the lime juice, and honey in a nonmetallic bowl, season with salt and pepper, and whisk by hand. Use a fork to mash in the avocado, then beat in the chiles, ginger, cilantro, and the remaining oil.

4. Adjust the seasoning, adding more honey or lime juice, if necessary. Serve immediately.

HERO TIPS

Unlike most hot sauces, this sauce is best eaten immediately, because the color will darken within 30 minutes of preparation.

FIERY & FIERCE GOCHUJANG SAUCE

Korean cooks used to make enough gochujang, a fermented chili and soybean paste, in the spring to last a family throughout the year. Use this sauce as a marinade or dipping sauce or for basting meat and poultry as they cook.

MAKES: ABOUT ⅔ CUP　　**PREP TIME: 5 MINS**　　**COOK TIME: NONE**

INGREDIENTS
⅓ cup gochujang paste
2 teaspoons chili paste
2 tablespoons sugar
2 tablespoons hot water
2 teaspoons light soy sauce
1 teaspoon rice vinegar
1 teaspoon toasted sesame oil

1. Combine the gochujang paste, chili paste, and sugar in a heatproof bowl, then add the water, stirring to blend, and dissolve the sugar and paste.

2. Stir in the soy sauce, vinegar, and sesame oil. Let cool completely.

3. Use the sauce immediately, or store it in an airtight container in the refrigerator for up to two weeks. If you want to make larger quantities, see page 10 for guidelines on longer storage.

HERO TIPS

This recipe combines authentic flavor with the speed of using the fermented bean and chili paste that is sold in plastic containers in many Asian supermarkets. No Korean barbecue or bibimbap is complete without it!

NOT-FOR-THE-FAINT-HEARTED NACHO SAUCE

This nacho sauce is creamy and smooth, with layers of heat from dry mustard, hot sauce, and finely chopped chiles. For nachos with heat, top tortilla chips with this sauce. It is also great mixed with cooked pasta or spooned over baked potatoes.

MAKES: ABOUT 1¼ CUPS   **PREP TIME: 5 MINS**   **COOK TIME: 15 MINS**

INGREDIENTS

1 cup shredded sharp cheddar cheese

3 tablespoons cornstarch

1 tablespoon dry mustard

1 cup milk

2 tablespoons cream cheese

2 teaspoons Louisiana Hot Pepper Sauce (see page 80), Spicy Sriracha Sauce (see page 92), or other hot sauce, to taste

2 red or green jalapeño chiles, finely chopped

salt and pepper, to taste

1. Mix together the cheese, cornstarch, and dry mustard in a heatproof bowl, then set aside.

2. Put the milk into a saucepan and bring just to a boil. Stir ¼ cup of the hot milk into the cheese mixture, stirring until well blended. Add the cheese mixture to the milk, whisking vigorously.

3. Return the mixture just to a boil, then reduce the heat and simmer, whisking frequently, for 5 minutes, until the cheese has melted and the sauce is smooth and has reduced. Remove the pan from the heat and stir in the cream cheese and hot sauce. Season with salt and pepper, then stir in the chiles.

4. Use the sauce immediately, or let it cool completely and store it in an airtight container in the refrigerator for up to three days. To serve, reheat gently without boiling.

HERO TIPS

Do not add the cornstarch or dry mustard directly to the hot milk or lumps will form. Whisk vigorously for a smooth mixture.

SCORCHING MOLE SAUCE

Toasted nuts and seeds make this classic Mexican sauce as rich as it is hot. The mixture of pasilla and ancho chiles creates a deep flavor that supports the heat. It's the chocolate, however, that is the essential ingredient in terms of its distinctive flavor.

MAKES: ABOUT 1½ CUPS   **PREP TIME: 15 MINS**   **COOK TIME: 10 MINS**

INGREDIENTS

3 tablespoons canola oil or sunflower oil

1 tablespoon shelled pumpkin seeds

1 day-old soft flour tortilla, broken into small pieces

1 red onion, chopped

1 teaspoon ground cinnamon

½ teaspoon cayenne pepper

½ teaspoon ground coriander

½ teaspoon ground cumin

¼ teaspoon ground cloves

3 dried pasilla chiles, toasted, soaked, stems and seeds removed (see page 82)

1 dried ancho chile, toasted, soaked, stem and seeds removed (see page 82)

¼ cup blanched almonds, toasted

¼ cup peeled hazelnuts, toasted

2 teaspoons sesame seeds, toasted

1 ounce bittersweet chocolate, chopped

salt and pepper, to taste

1. Heat 1 tablespoon of the oil in a skillet over medium–high heat. Add the pumpkin seeds and cook for 30–60 seconds, or until they start popping. Transfer to a food processor or blender.

2. Heat another tablespoon of oil in the skillet and quickly heat the tortilla pieces for 1 minute, or until golden. Add to the food processor.

3. Heat the remaining oil in the skillet. Add the onion and sauté for 3–5 minutes, or until soft. Add the spices and sauté for an additional minute.

4. Add the onion mixture to the food processor with the pasilla chiles, ancho chile, nuts, sesame seeds, and chocolate and season with salt and pepper. Process the sauce, scraping down the sides, if necessary, until a thick, grainy sauce forms. Adjust the seasoning, if necessary.

5. Use the sauce immediately, or let it cool completely and store it in an airtight container in the refrigerator for up to three days. You can freeze the sauce for up to one month; see page 10.

VOLATILE TERIYAKI SAUCE

Fiery green wasabi paste, known as Japanese horseradish, and fresh ginger give this traditional Japanese sauce a burst of heat, as well as extra flavor.

MAKES: ABOUT ⅓ CUP   **PREP TIME: 5 MINS**   **COOK TIME: 8-10 MINS**

INGREDIENTS

½ cup Japanese soy sauce
¼ cup sake
¼ cup mirin or dry sherry
¼ cup firmly packed brown sugar
1 garlic clove, crushed
1-inch piece fresh ginger
1 tablespoon green wasabi paste, or to taste

1. Combine the soy sauce, sake, mirin, sugar, and garlic in a saucepan, stirring to dissolve the sugar. Grate the ginger directly into the pan to capture all the juices. Bring to a boil, then reduce the heat and simmer, uncovered, for 8–10 minutes, or until thickened to a coating consistency.

2. Add the wasabi paste and stir until dissolved.

3. Use the sauce immediately, or let it cool completely and store it in an airtight container in the refrigerator for up to three weeks. Grate in the ginger only when you are ready to serve, then reheat the sauce.

INCANDESCENT CURRY SAUCE

This is a good sauce to make in large batches and freeze in convenient portions for future meals. This sauce is versatile enough to be used as the base for meat, poultry, and vegetable curries.

MAKES: ABOUT 1¼ CUPS   **PREP TIME: 10 MINS**   **COOK TIME: 20 MINS**

INGREDIENTS

1 (14½-ounce) can diced tomatoes

2–3 green or red Thai chiles, to taste, chopped

4 garlic cloves, chopped

½-inch piece fresh ginger, chopped

3 tablespoons peanut oil or sunflower oil

2 onions, finely chopped

1½ teaspoons salt

½ teaspoon turmeric

pinch of light brown sugar

1 tablespoon garam masala

pepper, to taste

1. Put the tomatoes, chiles, garlic, and ginger into a food processor or blender and puree. Alternatively, pound together the chiles, garlic, and ginger with a mortar and pestle, then pound in the tomatoes. Set aside.

2. Heat the oil in a large wok or saucepan over medium–high heat. Add the onions and sauté, stirring continuously, for 5–8 minutes, or until lightly browned. Add the tomato mixture and bring to a boil, stirring.

3. Stir in the salt, turmeric, and sugar and season with pepper. Reduce the heat to low and let simmer, uncovered, for 10–15 minutes, or until the oil separates around the edge of the sauce.

4. Stir in the garam masala and remove the sauce from the heat.

5. Use the sauce immediately, or let it cool completely and store it in an airtight container in the refrigerator for up to three days. You can freeze the sauce for up to three months; see page 10.

BLOW YOUR HEAD OFF!

PERI-PERI AT YOUR PERIL SAUCE

This peri-peri sauce is as good as any you would find at well-known restaurants! Pair this sauce with fried chicken wings for a hot and spicy meal.

MAKES: ABOUT ⅓ CUP   **PREP TIME: 10 MINS**   **COOK TIME: 10 MINS**

INGREDIENTS
¼ cup sunflower oil

24 peri-peri chiles or red Thai chiles, chopped

½ onion, finely chopped

4 large garlic cloves, chopped

1 teaspoon sweet paprika

¼ teaspoon ground allspice

⅓ cup freshly squeezed lemon juice, or to taste

2 tablespoons water

finely grated zest of 1 lemon

salt and pepper, to taste

1. Turn the extractor to high or open a window to let air circulate. Heat the oil in a saucepan over medium heat. Add the chiles and onion and sauté for 3 minutes. Add the garlic, paprika, and allspice and stir for an additional minute.

2. Add ¼ cup of the lemon juice and the water and season with salt and pepper. Bring to a boil, stirring. Reduce the heat to low, cover, and simmer for 5 minutes, or until the chiles are soft. Uncover and check once or twice to make sure the garlic doesn't burn.

3. If you would like a smooth, restaurant-style sauce, transfer the ingredients to a small food processor or blender and puree, or leave as a chunky sauce, if preferred. Stir in the remaining lemon juice. Adjust the seasoning and lemon juice, as desired. Stir in the lemon zest.

4. Use the sauce immediately, or let it cool completely and store it in an airtight container in the refrigerator for up to two weeks. For guidelines on longer storage, see page 10.

JAMAICAN JERK SIZZLING SAUCE

This hot, hot, hot Caribbean favorite can be used as a marinade or as a basting sauce while barbecuing. Chicken is its traditional partner, but it also adds a sunny Caribbean taste to most meat and seafood dishes.

MAKES: ABOUT 1¼ CUPS **PREP TIME: 10 MINS PLUS RESTING** **COOK TIME: NONE**

INGREDIENTS

¼ cup freshly squeezed lemon juice

¼ cup dark soy sauce

¼ cup sunflower oil

¼ cup red wine vinegar or white wine vinegar

4 red Scotch bonnet chiles or habanero chiles, seeded and minced

4 scallions, minced

1 shallot, minced

1-inch piece fresh ginger, grated

2 tablespoons firmly packed light brown sugar

2 teaspoons dried thyme

1 teaspoon ground allspice

½ teaspoon ground cinnamon

¼ teaspoon ground cloves

salt and pepper, to taste

1. Mix together the lemon juice, soy sauce, oil, and vinegar in a large nonmetallic bowl.

2. Stir in the remaining ingredients and season with salt and pepper, stirring until the sugar dissolves. Set aside for at least 30 minutes for the flavors to blend.

3. Use the sauce immediately, or store it in an airtight container in the refrigerator for up to one month.

LOUISIANA HOT PEPPER SAUCE

This sauce is traditionally made with fresh, small tabasco chiles, but they can be difficult to source, so dried cayenne or Thai chiles are used in this recipe to give the same tongue-tingling sensation.

MAKES: ABOUT ½ CUP   **PREP TIME: 5 MINS PLUS SOAKING**   **COOK TIME: 15 MINS**

INGREDIENTS

2 ounces dried red cayenne peppers or dried red Thai chiles, stems removed, coarsely chopped and soaked for 30 minutes (see page 82)

½ cup white wine vinegar

½ teaspoon salt

1. Turn the extractor to high or open a window. Drain the soaked chiles. Put the chiles, vinegar, and salt into a small saucepan. Cover the pan and bring to a boil, then reduce the heat to low and let simmer for 10–12 minutes, or until soft.

2. Transfer the contents of the pan to a small food processor or blender and puree, scraping down the sides, if necessary. Strain the blended mixture to remove the seeds. Transfer the sauce to a nonmetallic bowl and let cool completely.

3. Let the sauce mature for at least two weeks in an airtight container in the refrigerator before using. The sauce will then keep in the refrigerator for an additional month. For longer storage, see page 10.

ROASTING HOT CARIBBEAN SAUCE

Hot, hot, hot—hotter than the Caribbean sun! There are many recipes for hot sauces throughout the Caribbean, and this version is inspired by the pepper sauces from Trinidad. Use it as a marinade for barbecued and grilled food or stir into soups and stews for a chile sensation.

MAKES: ABOUT 1¼ CUPS   PREP TIME: 10 MINS   COOK TIME: 10 MINS

INGREDIENTS
8 red and/or orange Scotch bonnet chiles or habanero chiles, seeded

4 garlic cloves, finely chopped

1 carrot, sliced

1 onion, finely chopped

⅓ cup cider vinegar or red wine vinegar

1 tablespoon freshly squeezed orange juice or lime juice, or to taste

salt and pepper, to taste

1. Bring a small saucepan of lightly salted water to a boil. Add the chiles and blanch for 30 seconds, or until just soft. Use a slotted spoon to transfer them to a blender or food processor.

2. Return the water to a boil. Add the garlic, carrot, and onion and boil for 5–8 minutes, or until the carrot is soft. Drain the vegetables and add to the blender with the vinegar and orange juice and season with salt and pepper.

3. Puree the ingredients until a sauce forms. Pass the sauce through a fine strainer into a bowl, rubbing back and forth with a wooden spoon and scraping the bottom of the strainer to produce as much puree as possible. Adjust the seasoning, if necessary. Transfer to a bowl and let cool completely.

4. Let the sauce mature in an airtight container in the refrigerator for two weeks, shaking it occasionally. It will keep for an additional two weeks in the refrigerator. For guidelines on longer storage, see page 10.

TOAST IT!

Not all chiles are best eaten fresh! Dried chiles are often toasted before using to intensify their flavors ... and they can also be soaked to soften before blending. Both techniques are easy and well worth investigating.

TOASTING CHILES

Heat a dry skillet over medium heat. Add the dry chiles and heat until you can smell their aroma. Press large chiles, such as guajillos and pastillas, with a metal spatula against the hot surface until they slightly puff up and soften. Immediately remove them from the pan and set aside. Be careful to avoid overtoasting them or they will taste bitter.

Smaller chiles, such as pequin, should be stirred continuously so they don't burn.

Alternatively, put the chiles on a baking sheet and place in an oven preheated to 425°F for 5 minutes, or until they slightly puff up and soften.

SOAKING CHILES

Many recipes specify to soak chiles so they are soft enough to blend. Put them in a heatproof bowl and pour enough boiling water over them to cover. Let stand for 5 minutes, or until softened and flexible. Smaller chiles, such as Thais and chipotles, need to be weighed down with a small saucepan lid or heatproof plate to keep them submerged.

Strain the chiles well, then pat dry and remove the stems. Some recipes also suggest cutting the chiles open and removing the seeds.

TOASTING NUTS & SEEDS

Intensify the flavor of nuts and seeds by dry-frying them in a heavy saucepan, stirring continuously, until they turn golden brown. Watch closely because they can burn in the blink of an eye. As soon as you can smell the aroma, immediately remove them from the pan so the oils do not continue cooking and develop a bitter flavor.

TOP TIPS FOR TOASTING & SOAKING

• Save on dish washing—when a recipe specifies to toast and soak chiles, dry-fry them, then add water to the pan and bring to a boil. Turn off the heat and let the chiles soak until they soften.

• Never throw away the liquid you soak your chiles in. It's full of flavor and is great for giving a kick to soups, stews, and gravies. Let it cool, then transfer to an airtight container and store in the refrigerator. Or, for the really organized, freeze in an ice cube tray, then transfer the individual cubes to a freezer-proof bag.

• To save time when cooking, toast batches of chiles, nuts, and seeds and store them individually in airtight containers, ready to use next time.

DANGEROUS ADOBO SAUCE

Chipotle chiles are dried jalapeño chiles available in two forms, morita or meco, both of which can be used in this recipe. Meco chipotles give a smokier flavor that goes particularly well with slow-cooked meat dishes.

MAKES: ABOUT 1¼ CUPS   PREP TIME: 10 MINS   COOK TIME: 1½-1¾ HRS

INGREDIENTS

¼ cup tomato paste
2½ cups water
⅓ cup white wine vinegar
12 dried chipotle chiles, stems removed
4 garlic cloves, crushed
½ red onion, minced
2 tablespoons firmly packed light brown sugar
1 tablespoon ground cumin
1 tablespoon dried Mexican oregano or dried thyme
2 teaspoons hot smoked paprika
2 teaspoons cayenne pepper
½ teaspoon salt
pepper, to taste

1. Dissolve the tomato paste in the water and vinegar in a deep saucepan. Stir in the remaining ingredients and season with pepper. Cover and bring to a boil.

2. Uncover, reduce the heat to low, and simmer for 1¼–1½ hours, or until the chiles are soft and the sauce thickens.

3. Transfer the sauce to a blender or food processor and puree. Strain the sauce through a strainer into a bowl, rubbing back and forth with a wooden spoon and scraping the bottom of the strainer to produce as much puree as possible. Set aside to cool completely.

4. Use the sauce immediately, or store it in an airtight container in the refrigerator for up to three weeks. For guidelines on longer storage, see page 10.

BLISTERING BLACK BEAN SAUCE

The Sichuan peppercorns in this stir-fry sauce will produce a distinctive tingling sensation in your mouth. Look for the peppercorns, as well as the black beans, in Chinese food stores. Don't confuse these salty beans with the ones used in Caribbean and Latin American cooking.

MAKES: ABOUT ⅔ CUP   **PREP TIME: 10 MINS**   **COOK TIME: 5 MINS**

INGREDIENTS

2 tablespoons peanut oil or sunflower oil

2 ounces salted or fermented black beans

4 scallions, finely chopped

4 green Thai chiles, finely chopped

1 tablespoon Sichuan peppercorns, toasted and crushed

½-inch piece fresh ginger, finely grated

½ cup beef stock, chicken stock, or vegetable stock

¼ cup light soy sauce

1 tablespoon arrowroot, dissolved in 1 tablespoon water

1 teaspoon toasted sesame oil

pepper, to taste

1. Heat a wok over high heat. Add the oil and heat until hot. Add the beans, scallions, chiles, peppercorns, and ginger and cook for 2 minutes, using a wooden spoon to break up the beans.

2. Add the stock and soy sauce and season with pepper. Bring to a boil, stirring, then reduce the heat to low.

3. Stir in the arrowroot mixture and simmer, without boiling, for 1–2 minutes, or until the sauce is thick and shiny. Adjust the pepper, if necessary. Sprinkle with the sesame oil.

4. Use the sauce immediately, or let it cool completely and store it, with a thin layer of oil poured over the top, in an airtight container in the refrigerator for up to one week.

HERO TIPS

Use 1–2 tablespoons of the black bean sauce per portion of stir-fry. The sauce is especially good in a beef stir-fry with green bell peppers and mushrooms.

LONE STAR PERILOUS PEQUIN SAUCE

Texans take their hot sauces seriously and this isn't a sauce for the fainthearted. The native pequin chiles grow to less than 1 inch and are available all year round as small, rosy-red dried chiles. What they lack in size, they make up for in intense, searing heat.

MAKES: ABOUT 2½ CUPS   PREP TIME: 10 MINS   COOK TIME: 40 MINS

INGREDIENTS

1½ tablespoons dried pequin chiles

1 teaspoon cumin seeds, toasted

½ teaspoon coriander seeds, toasted

4 tomatoes, chopped

1 red onion, chopped

1 cup tomato puree or tomato sauce

¼ cup red wine vinegar

1 tablespoon molasses

2 teaspoons dried thyme

salt and pepper, to taste

1. Heat a skillet over high heat. Add the chiles and dry-fry, stirring, for 30–60 seconds, or until they start to brown. Immediately remove them from the pan. If they burn, they will taste bitter. Use a mortar and pestle or the back of a wooden spoon to finely crush the chiles and seeds.

2. Put the remaining ingredients in a saucepan, add the crushed chiles, and season with salt and pepper. Bring to a boil, stirring to dissolve the molasses. Reduce the heat to low, partly cover, and simmer for 30 minutes, stirring occasionally to prevent the sauce from sticking to the bottom of the pan.

3. Transfer the sauce to a food processor or blender and puree. Adjust the seasoning, if necessary.

4. Use the sauce immediately, or let it cool completely and store it in an airtight container in the refrigerator for up to one week. You can freeze the sauce for up to three months, see page 10.

VOLCANIC VINDALOO SAUCE

This blisteringly hot sauce derives from when the Portuguese introduced the hot chile and vinegar to Goa in the sixteenth century. If there is time, let the masala and crushed chile mixture stand for up to 4 hours in Step 2 for the flavors to intensify.

MAKES: ABOUT 2 CUPS   **PREP TIME: 15 MINS**   **COOK TIME: 35 MINS**

INGREDIENTS

2 tablespoons sunflower oil
1 onion, thinly sliced
4 large tomatoes, chopped
1 tablespoon dark brown sugar
1 teaspoon salt
½ cup water
pepper, to taste

VINDALOO MASALA

1-inch cinnamon stick
1½ teaspoons coriander seeds
½ teaspoon cumin seeds
½ teaspoon black mustard seeds
¼ teaspoon fennel seeds
¼ teaspoon black peppercorns
2 tablespoons red wine vinegar
1-inch piece fresh ginger, grated
5 dried red Thai chiles or cayenne chiles, finely chopped
2 large garlic cloves, crushed

1. To make the masala, heat a dry skillet over medium–high heat. Add the cinnamon, all the seeds, and the peppercorns and heat, stirring, for 1–2 minutes until aromatic. Immediately remove from the skillet and finely grind in a small food processor or using a mortar and pestle.

2. Transfer the crushed mixture to a nonmetallic bowl, stir in the vinegar, ginger, chiles, and garlic, and set aside.

3. Heat the oil in a heavy saucepan over low heat. Add the onion and sauté for 8–10 minutes, or until lightly browned.

4. Add the tomatoes, sugar, salt, masala mixture, and water and stir. Bring to a boil, then reduce the heat to low. Cover and simmer for 15 minutes, stirring occasionally to break down the tomatoes. Season with pepper.

5. Use the sauce immediately, or let it cool completely and store it in an airtight container in the refrigerator for up to one week.

SPICY SRIRACHA SAUCE

Homemade sriracha will never taste exactly the same as the store-bought version, because it contains no commercial stabilizers. However, this Thai-style favorite, thickened with a little arrowroot, has a delicious flavor with just the same chile hit.

MAKES: ABOUT ¾ CUP   **PREP TIME: 10 MINS PLUS STANDING**   **COOK TIME: 30 MINS**

INGREDIENTS

14 red jalapeño, serrano, or Fresno chiles, or a combination (about 8 ounces), stems removed and halved lengthwise

1 red Thai chile, seeded

8 garlic cloves, coarsely chopped

3 tablespoons packed light brown sugar

2 tablespoons granulated sugar

2 teaspoons salt

⅓ cup white wine vinegar

1 teaspoon arrowroot

1. Put all the ingredients, except the vinegar and arrowroot, into a food processor or blender and finely chop. Transfer to a screw-topped jar large enough to hold the mixture with space at the top and seal. Let stand at warm room temperature, shaking once a day, for two to four days, or until the mixture becomes liquid.

2. Return the mixture to the food processor, add the vinegar, and puree. Strain into a saucepan, rubbing back and forth with a spoon and scraping the strainer to produce as much puree as possible.

3. Turn the extractor to high, or open a window to let air circulate. Place the pan over medium heat, bring the puree to a boil, and stir until it is reduced by one-quarter. Reduce the heat to low.

4. Dissolve the arrowroot with 1 tablespoon of the hot liquid, then stir into the pan. Stir for 30 seconds, until the sauce thickens slightly. Set aside.

5. Let cool then let mature for two weeks in a covered container in the refrigerator. The sauce will keep for one month in the refrigerator. For guidelines on longer storage, see page 10.

FIERY GARLIC-PEPPER SAUCE

This sauce is ideal for adding punchy heat to slow-roasted pork belly, but is equally good in stir-fries and for brushing on chops or steaks before chargrilling.

MAKES: ABOUT ¾ CUP   **PREP TIME: 5 MINS**   **COOK TIME: 1 HR**

INGREDIENTS
10 red Thai chiles

2 red bell peppers, quartered and seeded

1 garlic bulb, about 12 cloves, separated

½ onion, chopped

1 teaspoon Chinese five spice

2 tablespoons sunflower oil

salt and pepper, to taste

1. Preheat the oven to 425°F.

2. Put the chiles, red bell peppers, garlic, and onion into a shallow ovenproof dish that holds them snugly. Sprinkle with the five spice, season with salt and pepper, then spoon the oil over the top and stir into the other ingredients. Cover the dish tightly with aluminum foil.

3. Place in the preheated oven and roast for 1 hour, or until all the vegetables are tender.

4. Transfer the vegetables and any cooking juices to a food processor or blender and puree. Pass the mixture through a fine strainer, rubbing back and forth with a wooden spoon and scraping the bottom of the strainer to produce as much puree as possible. Adjust the salt and pepper, if necessary.

5. Use the sauce immediately, or store it in an airtight container in the refrigerator for up to two weeks. For guidelines on longer storage, see page 10.

HOT-BLOODED HUNGARIAN PAPRIKASH SAUCE

Hungarians fortify themselves against cold winters with spicy-hot meat stews flavored with paprika. It comes in varying degrees of heat—this is the searing-hot version. For a quick taste of Hungary, pour this sauce over cooked chicken thighs and let simmer so the flavors blend.

MAKES: ABOUT 1½ CUPS   PREP TIME: 10 MINS   COOK TIME: 25 MINS

INGREDIENTS

1 teaspoon caraway seeds
2 tablespoons sunflower oil
1 large onion, thinly sliced
2 tablespoons hot Hungarian paprika
1¼ cups sour cream
1 tablespoon tomato paste
1 teaspoon dried dill
salt and pepper, to taste

1. Toast the caraway seeds in a dry skillet over medium–high heat for 1–2 minutes, or until aromatic. Transfer from the skillet to a bowl.

2. Add the oil to the skillet and heat. Add the onion and sauté for 3–5 minutes, or until soft. Stir in the paprika and cook for 30 seconds.

3. Stir in the sour cream and tomato paste and season with salt and pepper. Bring just to a boil, then reduce the heat to low and simmer for 10–15 minutes, stirring occasionally, until reduced. Stir in the caraway seeds and dill and adjust the seasoning, if necessary.

4. Use the sauce immediately, or let it cool completely and store it in an airtight container in the refrigerator for up to three days.

HERO TIPS

If the sauce thickens too much in the refrigerator, it can be thinned with a little chicken stock when added to meat and vegetables.

97

HOTTER-THAN-AN-OVEN HABANERO SAUCE

Don't be deceived by the initial sweet flavor. As this sauce hits the back of the tongue, the searing heat kicks in. Typical of many sauces from the Caribbean, this version mixes tropical fruit with habanero or Scotch bonnet chiles. Drizzle over freshly grilled seafood kabobs.

MAKES: ABOUT ¾ CUP   **PREP TIME: 10 MINS**   **COOK TIME: 25 MINS**

INGREDIENTS
8 green habanero or Scotch bonnet chiles, halved, 4 seeded

2 large green bell peppers, halved and seeded

3 tablespoons chopped fresh mango

1 white onion, finely chopped

¼ cup sugar dissolved in ¼ cup white wine vinegar

1-inch piece fresh ginger, grated

salt and pepper, to taste

1. Preheat the broiler to high and line a baking sheet with aluminum foil. Put the chiles and green bell peppers, cut side down, on the baking sheet and cook for about 10 minutes for the chiles and about 25 minutes for the green bell peppers, until charred and soft. Watch closely so they do not burn. Remove with tongs, transfer to a bowl, and cover with a clean dish towel.

2. When cool enough to handle, rub off the skins, then finely chop the flesh.

3. Transfer to a small food processor or blender with the remaining ingredients and season with salt and pepper. Blend until smooth. Strain the sauce through a fine strainer.

4. Use the sauce immediately, but is best if you let it mature in an airtight container in the refrigerator for at least two days before using. It will keep in the refrigerator for up to two weeks. For guidelines on longer storage, see page 10.

GROW YOUR OWN!

So we know you love the taste of chiles, but did you realize they're actually easy to grow yourself? You don't need to be living in a hot country or near the equator. With just a little care, anyone can nurture a crop!

And the best news? You don't need a yard—chiles are best grown in flowerpots, so any little amount of outdoor space should be enough, even a windowsill.

1. Plant in January to harvest in July, but start them off indoors. In cold regions, it's too cold outside for your chile plants until at least mid-May.

2. Fill a seed-starting flat with soil mix, lightly water, and place a seed in each compartment. Add a little more soil mix on top. Water again, cover with plastic wrap, and place somewhere warm.

3. After about a month, you should see some seeds sprouting. Remove the plastic wrap and move to a warm windowsill. Keep moist.

4. When your seedlings develop a second set of leaves, carefully transplant them to small flowerpots and encourage growth with a weekly balanced fertilizer.

5. At about 5 inches tall, transplant again to bigger flowerpots (or fit up to three in a really big container). Support drooping plants by tying to a stake.

6. Try not to let your plants grow much above a foot tall—pinch off the tops above the leaves to encourage bushiness and more flowers. Each flower should become a chile.

7. Snip off (and eat) the first crop while they're still green, to encourage regrowth, and you should be harvesting chiles all the way from July to October.

THE ULTIMATE HOT-AS-HELL CHILI SAUCE

Are you brave enough to try this? The ghost chile—also known as the naga chile and Bhut Jolokia—once reigned supreme as the world's hottest chile. Turn the extractor to high before boiling the sauce and be sure to wear rubber gloves when handling.

MAKES: ABOUT ¾ CUP

PREP TIME: 15 MINS PLUS STANDING

COOK TIME: 15 MINS

INGREDIENTS

1 tablespoon allspice berries, lightly crushed

1 tablespoon coriander seeds, toasted and lightly crushed

2 teaspoons cumin seeds, toasted

1 teaspoon fennel seeds, toasted

8 dried ghost (naga) chiles

2 dried habanero chiles

2 carrots, thinly sliced

1 celery stalk, chopped

1 small red onion, chopped

1½ cups cider vinegar

½ cup water, plus extra if needed

¼ cup firmly packed light brown sugar

2 red chargrilled peppers from a jar, chopped

1. Turn the extractor to high or open a window to let air circulate. Place the berries and seeds in a square of cheesecloth, gather together the sides, and tie into a bag, then place in a saucepan. Stir in all the chiles, the carrot, celery, onion, vinegar, and water, adding extra water to cover all the ingredients. Weigh down the chiles with a plate.

2. Bring to a boil and boil for 5 minutes. Remove from the heat, stir in the sugar, and let stand, covered, for at least 1 hour. Press the bag firmly with a spoon to extract as much flavor as possible.

3. Remove and discard the cheesecloth bag. Strain the remaining contents of the pan, then remove the chile stems. Transfer the chiles to a food processor with the red peppers, carrot, celery, and onion.

4. Puree and add 1–2 tablespoons of the cooking liquid. Pass the sauce through a strainer, rubbing back and forth with a spoon and scraping the strainer to produce as much puree as possible.

5. Let cool then let mature for two weeks in an airtight container in the refrigerator before using. It will keep for one month in the refrigerator. For guidelines on longer storage, see page 10.

SAUCY RECIPES!

TEXAS-STYLE BIG RED CHILI

Texans don't tolerate beans or any other additions in their big bowls of chili. What you see is what you get—just chunks of beef and hot chili sauce. It's plain and simple, and utterly delicious.

SERVES: 4   **PREP TIME: 10 MINS**   **COOK TIME: 3 HRS**

INGREDIENTS

2 tablespoons rendered bacon fat, sunflower oil, or canola oil, plus extra, if needed

1¾ pounds boneless chuck beef or round beef, cut into 1-inch cubes

1 large onion, finely chopped

1 large garlic clove, finely chopped

1 tablespoon crushed red pepper flakes

1 serving Texan Chili sauce (see page 54)

1 tablespoon masa harissa

1 tablespoon red wine vinegar

salt and pepper, to taste

cooked rice and sour cream, to serve

1. Heat the fat in a large, heavy saucepan over medium heat. Season the beef with salt and pepper. Working in batches, add the beef to the pan and cook, stirring occasionally, until brown on all sides, adding extra fat as needed. Set aside the beef and juices.

2. Pour off all but 1 tablespoon of the fat. Add the onion to the pan and sauté for 3–5 minutes, or until soft. Add the garlic and red pepper flakes and cook for an additional minute. Return the beef and all the juices to the pan and stir in the Texan Sauce. Cover and bring to a boil, then reduce the heat to low and simmer for 2¼–2½ hours, until the beef is tender.

3. Put the harissa into a small bowl and stir in the vinegar. Stir the mixture into the chili and simmer for 10 minutes, or until the chili thickens. Season to taste. Serve in bowls over rice, with sour cream.

HERO TIPS

All that's required to make this chili into a satisfying evening meal is some cooked rice or tortilla crisps on the side.

PULLED PORK BURRITOS

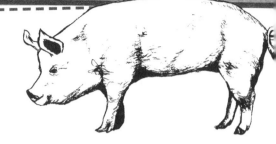

This is a recipe that takes its time to cook, but the end result is so delicious that it's worth it. A gentle, pleasing aroma of the chipotle chiles in the sauce fills the kitchen while the pork roasts slowly.

SERVES: 4   **PREP TIME: 10 MINS**   **COOK TIME: 6 HRS**

INGREDIENTS

1¾ pounds boneless pork shoulder

¼ cup tomato puree or tomato sauce

1 serving Chipotle & Lime Inferno Sauce (see page 48)

2 tablespoons chopped fresh cilantro

freshly squeezed lime juice, to taste (optional)

salt and pepper, to taste

TO SERVE

shredded crisp lettuce

8 soft flour tortillas

warmed guacamole (optional)

chopped scallions (optional)

chopped pickled jalapeños (optional)

Louisiana Hot Pepper Sauce (see page 80)

1. Preheat the oven to 425°F. Use a sheet of aluminum foil large enough to enclose the pork to line a baking pan, shiny side up.

2. Season the pork with salt and pepper and place in the middle of the foil. Pour over the tomato puree or sauce and half of the Chipotle & Lime Inferno Sauce. Wrap the foil around the meat and fold in the seams. Roast in the preheated oven for 30 minutes.

3. Reduce the oven temperature to 250°F. Roast for an additional 5 hours, or until the meat is soft when you squeeze the foil package. Remove from the oven and let rest, wrapped, for 20 minutes.

4. Heat the remaining sauce in a saucepan and add the cooking juices from the pork package. Discard the pork rind and fat. Use two forks to shred the meat, then stir into the sauce. Add the cilantro, and the lime juice, if using. Adjust the seasoning, if necessary.

5. Place the lettuce in the center of a tortilla, then add the pork mixture and chosen toppings. Top with the hot sauce and fold up the tortilla. Repeat with the other tortillas, then serve.

BLAZING HOT WINGS

Chicken wings are famous for being quick, easy and finger-lickingly tasty—and this recipe ticks all three boxes. To prepare ahead, coat the wings with the sticky marinade up to a day in advance.

SERVES: 4

PREP TIME: 10 MINS PLUS MARINATING

COOK TIME: 30-35 MINS

INGREDIENTS

4 tablespoons maple syrup

1 tablespoon Louisiana Hot Pepper Sauce (page 80)

24 chicken wings, wingtips removed and each wing cut into 2 pieces at the "elbow" joint

sunflower oil, for brushing

salt and pepper

BLUE CHEESE DRESSING

4 ounces blue cheese

1 tablespoon English mustard

1¼ cups sour cream

2 tablespoons finely snipped chives

salt and pepper

1. Combine the maple syrup and Louisiana Hot Pepper Sauce in a large bowl. Season with salt and pepper.

2. Add the chicken wings and rub in the sauce mixture. Set aside at room temperature for 30 minutes. If making in advance, cover the bowl with plastic wrap and chill in the refrigerator until 30 minutes before cooking.

3. When ready to broil, preheat the broiler to high. Line the rack with aluminum foil, shiny side up, and brush the rack with oil.

4. Arrange the chicken wing pieces on the rack, fleshy side down. Position the rack 5 inches from the heat and cook for 20 minutes, basting occasionally with any marinade left in the bowl.

5. Turn the chicken pieces over, baste and continue to cook for 10–15 minutes, or until the skin is dark golden brown and the juices run clear when the thickest part of the meat is pierced with a sharp knife.

6. Meanwhile, to make the dressing, blend the cheese, mustard, and sour cream in a small food processor or blender. Stir in the chives and season with salt and pepper. Cover and chill until required.

7. Serve the chicken wings hot, at room temperature or chilled, with the dressing on the side.

A WORLD OF FLAVOR

Although chiles originated in South and Central America, they are now grown in just about every part of the world—and have contributed to the many sauce flavors we now associate with particular regions.

SOUTH AMERICA

The home of the chile produces a traditionally mild cuisine—so the addition of a sauce is often needed to add a little fire. The most popular remains Adobo sauce, made from chiles, such as chipotle, with Mexican oregano, onions, and tomatoes; but almost every amateur chef will have his own recipe, often using chipotle or jalapeño chiles.

USA

Known simply as hot sauces, US flavors are made with chiles, vinegar, and salt—but often with the addition of fruits and vegetables as diverse as raspberries, mangoes, tomatoes, and carrots to mellow out the flavor or add a thick edge to the sauce. The most popular chiles used in US sauces are jalapeño, chipotle, habanero, and cayenne, and the results range from very mild barbecue sauces to the spicy hot pepper sauce—which can even be aged in wooden casks, like wine.

CARIBBEAN

Sauces made from chiles feature heavily in Caribbean cuisine and, like their US cousins, most are made with the addition of fruit and vegetables to temper the flavor. However, as most Caribbean sauces feature habanero and Scotch bonnet chiles, the results still tend to be far hotter! Homemade sauces are very common too, with flavors as strong as onions and garlic often added for extra piquancy.

EUROPE

Two of the hottest chili sauces in the world originate from the UK. Made from the Naga Viper and Infinity chiles, they remain a specialized taste for most as they are so hot. However, the Portuguese peri-peri sauce, made from crushed peri-peri chiles with lime, citrus peel, garlic, and various herbs, remains popular across the continent.

MIDDLE EAST

The ancients of this region believed that chiles held near-magical healing powers, and so much of the traditional cuisine features sauces with chiles as ingredients. The most popular remains harissa—made from fresh and dried hot chiles and seasoned with caraway seeds.

ASIA

As you might expect, chili sauces are very popular in Asia and used to flavor almost all of their native cuisine. Often made with the addition of beans, much Asian chili sauce is made as a thick paste, which can be added to curries, as a dipping sauce or for stir-frying.

JERK CHICKEN

Authentic Jamaican jerk chicken has a unique flavor from being slowly cooked over pimento, or allspice, wood. You might not be able to replicate the exact flavor at home, but this recipe gives you the heat of true Jamaican jerk.

SERVES: 4

PREP TIME: 10 MINS PLUS MARINATING

COOK TIME: 40 MINS

INGREDIENTS

4 chicken legs

1 serving of Jamaican Jerk Sizzling Sauce (see page 78)

sunflower oil, for brushing

coleslaw, pineapple, and rice salad, to serve (optional)

1. Use a fork to pierce the chicken legs all over. Place the chicken in a bowl in a single layer. Pour the Jamaican Jerk Sizzling Sauce over the meat and rub into the chicken pieces. Cover the bowl with plastic wrap and marinate in the refrigerator for at least 4 hours, or for up to 36 hours.

2. Remove the chicken from the refrigerator 30 minutes in advance of cooking. Light a barbecue and heat until the coals turn gray. Alternatively, preheat the broiler to high and oil the broiler rack.

3. Place the chicken pieces on the rack, fleshy side down. Brush with some of the sauce remaining in the bowl and cook for 20 minutes.

4. Turn the chicken over and cook for an additional 20 minutes, brushing with the remaining sauce, or until it is cooked through and the juices run clear when the thickest part of the flesh is pierced with a sharp knife.

5. Transfer the chicken to a warm plate and let rest for 5 minutes. Use a heavy knife to cut each leg into four pieces, then serve with coleslaw, pineapple, and rice salad, if using.

TURKEY MOLE

This is a great dish for entertaining because the sauce can be made up to five days in advance. One word of caution: Do not leave the simmering sauce unattended for long, because it will stick to the bottom of the pan.

SERVES: 4   **PREP TIME: 1-1¼ HRS**   **COOK TIME: 35 MINS**

INGREDIENTS

2 tablespoons sunflower oil or canola oil

1 red onion, finely chopped

4 garlic cloves, finely chopped

1 serving Scorching Mole Sauce (see page 70)

salt and pepper, to taste

chopped fresh cilantro and toasted pumpkin seeds, to garnish

cooked rice, to serve

MEXICAN TURKEY STOCK

2¾ pounds turkey pieces, such as legs and thighs, skinned

2 bay leaves

2 red chiles, chopped

2 onions, unpeeled and halved

several fresh cilantro sprigs, tied

1 teaspoon black peppercorns, lightly crushed

1 teaspoon coriander seeds, lightly crushed

1. To make the stock, put the turkey pieces into a large saucepan with enough water to cover. Bring to a boil and skim the surface. When the scum stops forming, add the remaining stock ingredients and season with salt. Bring the water to a boil, then reduce the heat to low, partly cover the pan, and simmer for 45 minutes–1 hour, or until the turkey is cooked through. Remove the turkey and set aside.

2. When the turkey is cool, remove the meat from the bones and cut into bite-size pieces. Set aside. Strain the stock into a bowl and set aside. Heat the oil in a large, heavy saucepan over medium heat. Add the onion and sauté for 3–5 minutes, or until soft. Add the garlic and sauté for another minute.

3. Add the Mole Sauce and ⅔ cup of the stock and bring to a boil. Reduce the heat to low and stir in the turkey until it is coated in sauce.

4. Let the mole simmer for 15–20 minutes, or until the sauce reduces. Adjust the seasoning, if necessary. Garnish with chopped cilantro and toasted pumpkin seeds and serve with rice.

SHRIMP & CHICKEN GUMBO

The Creole-style gumbo originated in Louisiana in the eighteenth century. Serve this recipe with a bowl of Louisiana Hot Pepper Sauce or harissa on the table for diners who just can't get enough heat.

SERVES: 4　　　　**PREP TIME: 10 MINS**　　　　**COOK TIME: 30 MINS**

INGREDIENTS

2 tablespoons sunflower oil or corn oil

½ red onion, thinly sliced

4 ounces spicy sausage, such as chorizo, skinned and chopped

1 pound skinless, boneless chicken thighs, cut into bite-size pieces

1 serving Creole Gumbo Flamin' Sauce (see page 50)

⅔ cup chicken stock or vegetable stock

1 pound large, cooked peeled shrimp

salt and pepper, to taste

chopped scallions, to garnish

cooked rice and Louisiana Hot Pepper Sauce (see page 80) or Feel-The-Heat Harissa (see page 52), to serve

1. Heat the oil in a large saucepan over medium–high heat. Add the onion and sauté for 3–5 minutes, or until soft. Add the sausage and cook until brown all over.

2. Add the chicken and cook for 1–2 minutes, or until lightly browned.

3. Add the Creole Gumbo Sauce and stock and bring to a boil. Reduce the heat to low and simmer, uncovered, for 15–20 minutes, or until the chicken is cooked through and tender.

4. Increase the heat, add the shrimp, and stir for 2–3 minutes, or until the shrimp are cooked through. Adjust the seasoning, if necessary.

5. To serve, put a mound of rice in the middle of four bowls and ladle the gumbo around each mound. Garnish with chopped scallions and serve immediately, with Louisiana Hot Pepper Sauce or Feel-The-Heat Harissa on top.

MEATBALLS IN ADOBO SAUCE

When you're expecting chile lovers for dinner, this is a great quick and easy dish to serve. The sauce is spicy hot and any leftovers make a great taco filling.

SERVES: 4   **PREP TIME: 20 MINS**   **COOK TIME: 20-25 MINS**

INGREDIENTS

½ cup dried bread crumbs

3–4 tablespoons milk

3 tablespoons all-purpose flour, for dusting

8 ounces lean ground round or ground sirloin beef

8 ounces ground pork

4 large garlic cloves, finely chopped

2 eggs, beaten

3 tablespoons finely chopped fresh parsley or cilantro

1 teaspoon ground cinnamon

1 teaspoon sweet paprika

¼ cup sunflower oil, for frying, plus extra if needed

1 serving Dangerous Adobo Sauce (see page 84)

1 cup coarsely chopped mozzarella cheese

¼ cup shredded cheddar cheese

salt and pepper, to taste

1. Combine the bread crumbs and milk in a bowl and let soak for 10 minutes. Put the flour on a plate and set aside. Preheat the oven to 400°F.

2. Combine the beef, pork, garlic, eggs, parsley, cinnamon, and paprika with the bread crumb mixture in a large bowl. Season with salt and pepper and stir to combine.

3. Using wet hands, shape the mixture into 24 equal-size balls. Heat the oil in a large skillet over medium heat. Working in batches, lightly roll the meatballs in the flour, shaking off the excess. Add the meatballs and cook, turning, until brown all over, then transfer to a baking dish.

4. Pour the Adobo Sauce over the meatballs in the dish, then sprinkle with the mozzarella cheese and cheddar cheese. Bake in the preheated oven for 15–20 minutes, or until the meatballs are cooked through, the sauce is hot, and the cheese is melting.

5. Meanwhile, preheat the broiler to high. Place the dish under the broiler and brown for 2–3 minutes.

BROILED TERIYAKI SALMON

The heat of the wasabi paste in this marinade will surprise most aficionados of Japanese food and delight everyone who enjoys food that wakes up the taste buds. This simple recipe makes an elegant main dish.

SERVES: 4

PREP TIME: 5 MINS PLUS MARINATING

COOK TIME: 10 MINS

INGREDIENTS

4 salmon fillets, each about 1 inch thick

1 serving of Volatile Teriyaki Sauce (see page 72)

sunflower oil, for greasing and brushing

salt and pepper, to taste

toasted sesame seeds and a mixed salad, to serve

1. Put the salmon into a nonmetallic bowl and rub the sauce into the fillets. Season with salt and pepper. Let marinate for at least 1 hour, or for up to 3 hours, if possible.

2. Preheat the broiler to high. Grease the rack with the oil and position the rack about 4 inches from the heat.

3. Put the fillets on the rack, skin side up, brush with any marinade remaining in the bowl, and cook for 4 minutes.

4. Gently turn over the fillets, brush again with any remaining marinade, and cook for an additional 4–6 minutes, or until the salmon is cooked through and flakes easily.

5. Let rest for a few minutes, then sprinkle with the sesame seeds and serve with the mixed salad.

HERO TIPS

Use any leftover sauce to drizzle over the cooked salmon if it is first heated until piping hot. If the sauce is too thick, thin it with a little sake.

PERI-PERI CHICKEN

Peri-peri restaurants have red-hot charcoal grills that produce a crisp finish to the chicken skin. This recipe creates a lightly charred skin with all the flavor of the restaurant version.

SERVES: 4-6

PREP TIME: 20 MINS PLUS MARINATING

COOK TIME: 40 MINS

INGREDIENTS

4 cups water, plus extra, if needed

1 tablespoon sea salt

2 bay leaves

2 garlic cloves, chopped

1 red or green jalapeño chile, thinly sliced

1 small bunch fresh thyme

3½-pound chicken, butterflied

sunflower oil, for greasing

1 serving Peri-Peri At Your Peril Sauce (see page 76)

salt and pepper, to taste

1. Put the water into a large, nonmetallic bowl with the salt, bay leaves, garlic, chile, and thyme. Submerge the chicken in the water, pushing the flavorings underneath. Cover with plastic wrap and marinate in the refrigerator for 8–24 hours.

2. Remove the chicken from the liquid 30 minutes before you want to cook it, then rinse under cold running water and dry completely. Set aside.

3. Meanwhile, preheat the broiler to high. Line the broiler pan with aluminum foil, brush the rack with oil, and position it 5 inches from the heat.

4. When ready to cook, rub half the Peri-Peri At Your Peril Sauce onto both sides of the chicken. Place the chicken on the rack, breast side down, and cook for 20 minutes, brushing once with some of the remaining sauce.

5. Turn the chicken over, brush with more sauce, and cook for an additional 15–20 minutes, basting once or twice, until the skin is lightly charred and the juices run clear when the thickest part of the meat is pierced with a sharp knife. Let rest for 5 minutes, then sprinkle with salt and pepper, cut into individual portions, and serve.

RED-HOT BEEF FAJITAS

These Tex-Mex fajitas get a new lease of life with fresh Red-Hot Green Sauce. This is a great dish for entertaining, because both the marinated beef and the sauce can be prepared ahead. What could be easier?

SERVES: 4

PREP TIME: 15 MINS PLUS MARINATING

COOK TIME: 10-15 MINS

INGREDIENTS

4 large garlic cloves, coarsely chopped

1 teaspoon ancho chili powder or other chili powder

1 pound skirt steak, in one piece

¼ cup freshly squeezed lime juice

2 tablespoons sunflower oil

1 large red onion, thinly sliced

2 green bell peppers, seeded and thinly sliced

2 red bell peppers, seeded and thinly sliced

salt and pepper, to taste

TO SERVE

shredded crisp lettuce

8 soft flour tortillas, warmed

Red-Hot Green Sauce, to taste (see page 58)

sour cream (optional)

shredded cheddar cheese (optional)

1. Crush the garlic and chili powder into a paste using a mortar and pestle.

2. Put the steak into a nonmetallic bowl and rub both sides with the lime juice, then rub in the garlic paste. Cover and marinate in the refrigerator for at least 8 hours, ideally for 24 hours, rubbing the marinade into the meat once or twice. Remove from the refrigerator 30 minutes before cooking.

3. Heat the oil in a skillet. Add the onion and sauté for 3 minutes. Add the green and red bell peppers, season with salt and pepper, and sauté for another 3–5 minutes, or until soft. Set aside and keep warm.

4. Meanwhile, heat a ridged, cast iron pan over high heat. Add the beef and cook for 3 minutes on each side for medium–rare. Let rest for 5 minutes, then cut into thin slices across the grain.

5. To assemble each fajita, place a row of shredded lettuce in the center of a tortilla, then top with the bell pepper and onion mixture, beef, and Red-Hot Green Sauce. Add sour cream and shredded cheese, if using. Fold up the bottom of the tortilla, then fold over the sides, burrito style, and serve immediately.

INDEX